THE LUCKY MAN

Borgo Press Books by MICHEL BARON

The Lucky Man

THE LUCKY MAN

A PLAY IN FIVE ACTS

MICHEL BARON

Translated and Adapted by Frank J. Morlock

THE BORGO PRESS
MMXIII

THE LUCKY MAN

Copyright © 1991, 2013 by Frank J. Morlock

FIRST BORGO PRESS EDITION

Published by Wildside Press LLC

www.wildsidebooks.com

DEDICATION

To the memory of my late friend, Arne Parma, whose power over women exceeded even that of Cadwell.

CONTENTS

CAST OF CHARACTERS 9
ACT I 11
ACT II 45
ACT III 81
ACT IV 117
ACT V 151
ABOUT THE TRANSLATOR 183

CAST OF CHARACTERS

Cadwell

Bendish

Laura

Olivia

Arabella

Selina

Worthy

Slice

Mr. Martin

Jenny

Little Gentleman

Three lackeys or pages

ACT I

The time is 1687. A large room in Olivia's house in London.

Olivia:

Yes, brother, your plan to marry Laura will not work unless someone opens her eyes about Cadwell.

Jenny:

(to Worthy) She loves him—you are not unaware of that. Laura is a widow, and I am certain that, if she isn't brought to reason, and very quickly, she won't delay marrying Cadwell. Count on what I tell you: I've been with her for several years and I know her.

Olivia:

(to Worthy) Aside from your little love interest, what would her uncle Victor think if he found she were married without being forewarned? Wouldn't he have a right to complain of us after having taken care to lodge her with us so we could watch her conduct and report to him?

Worthy:

I see all this as you see it, but my love makes me say more than I should. I'm afraid of displeasing Laura, and besides—

Jenny:

(interrupting him) And while we debate these matters Cadwell perhaps will marry Laura.

Worthy:

(to Olivia) What must I do then?

Olivia:

Fulfill your promise to Victor to warn him of all that is happening. Tell him of your passion for his niece. Omit nothing that might serve to render you happy.

Worthy:

I could never do it.

Jenny:

What! Such false delicacy—

Worthy:

But, sis, please—

Olivia:

(interrupting him) Brother, do you want to marry Laura or not?

Worthy:

Yes, I mean to do it!

Olivia:

Then do what you're told and we will take care of the rest.

Worthy:

My happiness is in your hands.

Jenny:

Get going then!

(Exit Worthy, looking very uncertain and ill at ease)

Olivia:

Jenny, what's Laura doing?

Jenny:

I've just finished dressing her. She'll soon be here.

Olivia:

We've got to find a way to expose this fine Mr. Cadwell.

Jenny:

Fine! He can be easily exposed and trapped. But I warn you, he'll get out of it again with a facility that will surprise you.

Olivia:

In spite of all that, Jenny, we must help my brother. You have promised me.

Jenny:

I haven't started badly, and while Cadwell has been in the country these last two days believe you me, I've not forgotten to rouse Laura's suspicions.

Olivia:

Here she is—

(Enter Laura)

What's wrong with you then, madam? You look sad to

me.

Laura:

I don't know, Olivia, I haven't slept.

Olivia:

The people who trouble your repose may not care to restore it to you.

Laura:

(defensively) You are very good, madam, to take part in something that regards me.

Olivia:

I admit to you that I would like to see you at ease.

(Laura turns her head towards Cadwell's apartment)

How little attention you pay to what I say to you! One must be more your friend than I am—

Laura:

(interrupting her) Not at all, Olivia. It seems to me I hear you—and if I were not to, should you be taking note of what I am doing?

Olivia:

Yes, I ought to, Laura. Don't I have an interest in everything that touches you? Do you imagine I can watch with pleasure as people abuse your good faith? Am I not aware of your unjust preference, and ought I not to try to make you know the difference between hearts that are truly attached to you and those that—? Believe me, Laura, I know it, and you will know them as I do, those who love you for yourself, those who sacrifice—

Laura:

(to Jenny, turning again towards Cadwell's apartment) Jenny, have you seen—?

Olivia:

Madam, I see that I am embarrassing you—

Laura:

Olivia, I ask your pardon. I admit to you—

Olivia:

(interrupting her) I will leave you—

Laura:

(trying to hold her) Oh, no—please—

(Exit Olivia)

Jenny:

It's clear that you have some distractions—

Laura:

(interrupting) Jenny!

Jenny:

Madam?

Laura:

Has he gone?

Jenny:

Who?

Laura:

Has he gone, I said?

Jenny:

Mr. Worthy?

Laura:

No.

Jenny:

Your lackey?

Laura:

Who spoke of my lackey? Cadwell—has he left?

Jenny:

I don't think he's awake yet.— For some time, you've become so difficult to serve that it requires far greater penetration and patience than I can muster to stand you. Am I the mistress of your distractions and caprices? People don't say I am the reason you are not loved?

Laura:

Jenny?

Jenny:

Madam?

Laura:

Would you kindly shut up?!

Jenny:

No, madam! Really, it's not my fault if Cadwell has spent two days without seeing you. How badly infatuated you are with that little villain!

Laura:

Jenny!

Jenny:

Madam?

Laura:

Once more, would you kindly shut up?

Jenny:

No, madam. You've spoken to me and I am responding, and I will speak.

Laura:

Well! Jenny, I forbid you to shut up. I don't know what way to prevent you from speaking.

Jenny:

You know the doctor told me yesterday, in front of you, that I have a plethora of words so excessive, that if I don't say something— You see, madam, silence is mortal to me.

Laura:

(with exasperation) Oh—speak, Jenny!

Jenny:

Ah, I feel better already. Tell me, madam, at the time you used to bore my head with exaggerating the happy state of widowhood, and how nothing in the world would induce you to remarry, had someone told you a man would come to propose to be your husband or lover (one doesn't make much distinction between the two these days), a restless man, always bizarre, always content with himself, never content with others—what would you have said?

Laura:

They would have violently offended me.

Jenny:

Oh, not offended. If that was so, you would feel the outrage and the shame you receive.

Laura:

Me?

Jenny:

You, madam. Don't you love Cadwell? It is his portrait

I have just drawn.

Laura:

How you paint him, Jenny!

Jenny:

As he is, madam, and as he ought to appear to you. While he wanted to please you and be loved by you, Cadwell was the finest man in the world. But as soon as he saw you would be faithful and loving, has he shown the least regard for you? What haven't you done for him? Think, madam, that you owe yourself something. You will pardon me for the liberty I am about to take. What would you think of an amiable young man, without wealth, lodging with you in the name of your uncle, and who has never been in a condition to make expenditures but for your love of him. I wish that this plan to marry him can justify your conduct, but in delaying, you permit people to think, to talk. And slowly but surely you're getting a reputation that doesn't do you much honor. I believe, I'd even swear, that your passion hasn't gone beyond looks and words. But Laura, is everyone obliged to believe as I do? The world is not good. Passion has often led others farther than you have gone. Think of your reputation, and your peace of mind.

(Laura rises and walks off)

But madam, where are you going?

Laura:

I don't know. Is Cadwell awake yet? Go to him—question him—his actions, his remarks, and report to me his every word.

Jenny:

Useless effort. I will always be misunderstood if I don't take constant pains. She's loyal and amorous—

(Exit Laura)

(Ender Bendish, from Cadwell's apartment)

Jenny:

Ah, there you are. What are you looking for?

Bendish:

(amiably) For a crazy lady, and I've found you. Now, I'm not looking anymore, as you see.

Jenny:

And aren't you a nasty impertinent fellow! Can I see your master?

Bendish:

No, it isn't wake-up time for him yet. After having wasted all his time in an armchair at his toilet, he still has half an hour to sleep, my word.

Cadwell:

(calling from his room) Hey, hey, Bendish!

Bendish:

Sir.

Jenny:

I will return in a moment.

Bendish:

You don't like nudity, I can see that. Wait, help me, I beg you to carry the toilet here.

Jenny:

Why?

Bendish:

He says it reeks in his chamber.

Jenny:

I'm afraid it reeks in his hair more than in his room.

(Bendish and Jenny take a toilet, which is at the entrance to Cadwell's chamber, and place it in a corner of the stage)

Cadwell:

(calling again from his room) Come on then, hey!

Bendish:

Coming! Yells like a devil. Don't people say he has a lot of business.

(Exit Jenny to Laura's apartment)

(Cadwell enters)

Cadwell:

Will you ever come?

Bendish:

I'm here.

Cadwell:

What time is it?

Bendish:

Doesn't matter.

Cadwell:

Scoundrel! Hasn't anyone come to ask for me?

Bendish:

Arabella's valet is waiting for you to wake up.

Cadwell:

Selina hasn't sent around?

Bendish:

I protect you from gossip. (drawing a letter and a watch from his jacket and presenting them to Cadwell) Here's a letter and a watch Selina sent you. Her lackey is going to come for a reply.

Cadwell:

Just put them there.

Bendish:

Aren't you going to read her letter?

Cadwell:

No. I know everything that will be in it.

Bendish:

(hearing a noise) Someone's knocking on the door. Shall I open it?

Cadwell:

See who it is!

(Bendish goes to open)

Ah, it's from Arabella.

(Enter Arabella's Lackey)

Lackey:

(giving a clasp to Cadwell) Yes, sir. Here is what madam sends you. Will you send a reply?

Cadwell:

A reply? No.

Lackey:

Will you come to her, sir?

Cadwell:

No.

Lackey:

Tomorrow perhaps, sir?

Cadwell:

Er—one of these days, certainly. (to Bendish) Hey, Bendish—haven't you got a watch? (Bendish gives Cadwell the watch, which Cadwell in turn presents to the lackey) Take this to your mistress. (to Bendish) Well now—finish dressing me.

(The Lackey bows and exits)

Bendish:

And what will Selina say when she doesn't see her watch anymore?

Cadwell:

Didn't I tell you to dress me?

Bendish:

Eh! You don't intend to go out?

Cadwell:

I don't know what I will do. I'd like to spend the day here. No, I have to go out. (Thinking he hears a noise) Someone's knocking. Another lackey, I'll bet.

Bendish:

No, sir, nobody's knocking.— Admit that it's a tiresome distinction to be a pretty fellow and not to be able to take a step without being run after by half the world. These are the perils one faces when one is made like you.

Cadwell:

There are times when I wish not to be as I am—when I'd give anything in the world to be like you.

Bendish:

I believe it.

Cadwell:

Perhaps you have some secret to make me disliked?

Bendish:

I do, sir. And it's very easy. You have only to continue to live the way you live, and I guarantee you the hate and scorn of all mankind. (hearing knocking) They're knocking.

Cadwell:

Open.

Bendish:

(after having opened the door) It's from Selina.

(Enter Selina's Lackey)

Lackey:

Sir, I've brought a letter and a watch.

Cadwell:

I know what it is. Here, give her this. (giving the Lackey the clasp)

(Exit Lackey)

Bendish:

He pipes with the flute and tunes with the drum.

Cadwell:

You seem quite astonished?

Bendish:

Me? No. I find this the best thing in the world. To love her today and betray her tomorrow. To take from one to give to the other. False confidences, slander, letters, sacrifices, flatteries, scandal—mere nothings! I am ready for everything. We won't be rich in the end, but we'll have a good laugh, right, sir?

Cadwell:

Ah, I'm delighted to see you reasonable.

Bendish:

Oh, sir, when a devil and a hermit live together, either the devil becomes a hermit or the hermit becomes a devil, I am absolutely convinced. Well, let's see who the unfortunate lady will be whose reputation you will ruin by some new perfidy. I can clearly see that your feelings are reserved for the Marquise.

Cadwell:

Which one?

Bendish:

Why, the one you long ago swore to be faithful to.

Cadwell:

No. I no longer love her.

Bendish:

Your flames are not more vehement for this good lady to whom I carried your portrait that same day?

Cadwell:

Ah, fie! I cannot suffer her. She paints!

Bendish:

And the other one—her best friend?

Cadwell:

She has no wit.

Bendish:

And the lawyer's widow?

Cadwell:

She isn't rich.

Bendish:

And her sister?

Cadwell:

She cannot stand the odor of tobacco.

Bendish:

The odor of tobacco? My God! Of all these ladies there isn't one over whom you haven't troubled my head. "Ah, Bendish, tell me she's totally charming. I will love her all my life. I will suffer a thousand deaths rather than even think of changing—" I hear you, I look at her, I examine her, I conclude you are right. The next day, I am a fool. She lacks a delicate heart. Her manners are rude; she loves you too much; she is jealous, or too indifferent; she cannot stand the odor of tobacco. You always find some fault in them to justify YOUR inconstancy.

Cadwell:

What do you care?

Bendish:

Huh? What do I care? You don't consider the false oaths I've taken time and again.

Cadwell:

Why do you do that?

Bendish:

To reestablish your tottering reputation.

Cadwell:

Who placed it in your care?

Bendish:

Oh! Oh! This isn't bad. Who made it my duty, you say?

Cadwell:

Yes?

Bendish:

My honor?

Cadwell:

The honor of Bendish?

Bendish:

Assuredly. You wouldn't have me confirm your reputation as the most rascally, the most vain, the most faithless, the least amorous man in the world, would you?

Cadwell:

It wouldn't please me at all.

Bendish:

Eh! What would you have me reply to such accusations? For you're seeing only the rough draft of the portrait they paint of you these days. What would you have me say?

Cadwell:

Nothing. Be quiet—and begin now.

Bendish:

Oh, sir, he who says nothing, admits, and I do not want anyone in the world to believe that I know your character; and besides, I plan to improve my business and yours, for you see everyone thinks of his own self-interest. I need only be silent in response to the hundred questions put to me. "My poor Bendish," said one. "Here's a finger ring. I beg you tell me what your master's up to. What time does he come in? What's he like when he doesn't see me? Does he think of me? Does he speak to you of me? Is he restless, happy, sad, gay, melancholy, at ease, taciturn, giddy, chagrined, joking, wise, crazy?" What the devil do I know—a hundred thousand other things of a like nature?

Cadwell:

Well—what do you reply to all this?

Bendish:

According to the ring.

Cadwell:

Ah! I know quite well that with you my honor and yours march quite separately—according to your interest.— Let's change the subject. Do you know what?

Bendish:

What?

Cadwell:

I believe I'm in love.

Bendish:

What! In love? Love in good faith?

Cadwell:

Yes, I tell you, in love.

Bendish:

But are you talking seriously?

Cadwell:

Must I give myself to the Devil for you to believe me?

Bendish:

And Laura?

Cadwell:

Oh! Laura, Laura! She's not aware of it.

Bendish:

Better for you. But tell me—how long will it last?

Cadwell:

You ask me too much. As if one could respond to that?

Bendish:

Do I know her?

Cadwell:

You know her.

Bendish:

You must have loved her for only a short time—for I've never heard you speak of her.

Cadwell:

Uh—a little while.

Bendish:

Is she pretty? Good! Plague on the fool for asking it. You will tell me shortly. Where does she reside? Far from here?

Cadwell:

No.

Bendish:

Better still. For in the beginning of these things, it's devilishly tiresome to carry three letters back and forth day in day out.

Cadwell:

No trouble to do it. You can do it without going out.

Bendish:

How's that?

Cadwell:

She resides here.

Bendish:

Is it Olivia?

Cadwell:

You have said it.

Bendish:

Ah, sir—!

Cadwell:

(interrupting him) What's wrong with you?

Bendish:

Have you considered carefully what you are doing?

Cadwell:

Very carefully.

Bendish:

Olivia is a friend of Laura. In her sight. You cannot be thinking or you intend to lose everything. Eh, sir, where is the probity, the honor. Think, I tell you—

Cadwell:

(interrupting him) I love moralizing. It puts me to sleep.

Bendish:

(seeing Jenny appear) Hold, sir. Here's Jenny. Instruct

her in all these plans.

(Enter Jenny)

Cadwell:

Eh, good day, Jenny. What do you want?

Jenny:

To bid you good day, sir. I have to speak to you for madam.

Cadwell:

(to Bendish) My jerkin. (Cadwell dresses throughout this scene without listening to Jenny)

Jenny:

If I hadn't believed myself able to do you and madam a service, sir, I wouldn't undertake to speak to you. I flatter myself you will find what I have to say agreeable. You know I am in your interests. It pains me to see that you don't wish to be happy. What wouldn't I give to see you make serious reflections on your humor. As for me, I believe you too honest a man not to reproach yourself sometimes for your conduct towards Laura.

Cadwell:

My watch.

Jenny:

Dare one tell you that dividing your love between twenty coquettes makes you neither more attractive nor more happy? Your feelings should be faithful to the most loveable lady in the kingdom. Believe me, sir, and you will be believing an affectionate girl totally in your interests. Be happy while you can. There will come a time when the desire to be happy will only meet with despair. You will not always be attractive, and you won't always find a Laura to love you.

Cadwell:

My sword.

Jenny:

Fifty thousand francs and Laura! In these days a pretty sum. It ought to be very tempting to you—and I don't know anybody else who wouldn't be tempted by all that.

Cadwell:

My purse.

Jenny:

Truly sir, it's useless for you to say or do something, to put to use the merit you have, and you have great merit if one believes the consensus—I intend to become the greatest lady in Paris if I can get you to fifty thousand francs and Laura.

Cadwell:

My wig.

Jenny:

What I am saying to you must be very unpleasant, for you not to reply one word to me.

Cadwell:

How do I look, Jenny?

Jenny:

Oh! Not very good at all. You enrage me.

Cadwell:

My gloves, my hat. (to Jenny) Goodbye, Jenny. (to Bendish as he leaves) Hey, Bendish.

Bendish:

Sir?

Cadwell:

(whispering in Bendish's ear) Listen.

(Exit Cadwell)

Jenny:

(aside) On my oath, there's a villainous man. (to Bendish) And you, you imagine that I am used to your coldness and lack of love?

Bendish:

I love moralists—they put me to sleep.

Jenny:

Go, go, traitor, I will teach you.

Bendish:

(interrupting her) You don't know what you are saying.

Jenny:

What, a girl like me, a man like you? Rascal. Infamous!

Bendish:

Leave, leave these pretty names, these illustrious names, to the unworthy master I serve—give me softer ones, more agreeable.

Jenny:

Give you sweet names!

Bendish:

Ah, pardon, child. I have my head full of Cadwell's follies.

Jenny:

(interrupting him) And your own?

Bendish:

That without thinking what I do—

Jenny:

(interrupting him) Very obliging way of justifying yourself. I will hold you to account.

Bendish:

I will reply with the same words he said to me when I tried to censure his conduct.

Jenny:

I believe it. You know that I have my complaints about you, and that I find you very bad—

Bendish:

How do I look, Jenny?

Jenny:

Ah, traitor! You copy Cadwell. But don't think that I am crazy enough to copy Laura.

Bendish:

Goodbye, child. I bid you good day.

Jenny:

Plague on the fool!

CURTAIN

ACT II

The scene is the same as in Act I. It's a short time later.

Lackey:

I'm going to find out if one can see, madam.

Arabella:

Eh! My child—tell me a bit, I beg you, Cadwell—is he here?

Lackey:

I don't know. I don't believe so. Shall I ring, madam?

Arabella:

Yes, ring. (Lackey pulls a bell cord) (Aside) Where can Cadwell be? His conduct doesn't satisfy me anymore. He has the gift of tasting everything he finds agreeable the very moment he finds it. And the lack of promptness he shows to see me ruins the pleasure I got from the watch he sent me this morning.

(Enter Jenny)

Jenny:

(to Lackey) Well! Who the devil made you ring so loud?

Lackey:

(exiting) One asks for madam.

Arabella:

(to Jenny) What's Laura doing?

Jenny:

She hasn't slept for the whole night. She's just been drowsing for a whole hour. If you wish, I will go tell her—

Arabella:

(interrupting) No, Jenny, I will wait till she wakes.

Jenny:

Or till Cadwell returns?

Arabella:

Why Cadwell?

Jenny:

To keep you company while waiting for Laura.

Arabella:

I've nothing to do with Cadwell.

Jenny:

And now, madam, pardon me for speaking so freely, there's a rumor about that you don't hate him—

Arabella:

Me?

Jenny:

All the world says that he loves you, at least.

Arabella:

All the world has lied, Jenny. It is true that certain understandings between people do result in passions. I hold myself no more guilty of loving him than of having inspired love. Really, when you hear such foolishness— But who can take pleasure in spreading rumors like that? Cadwell himself hasn't any part in it?

Jenny:

Why, madam—what stops you? What makes you angry today is the glory of most women. And the pleasure of being told they are loved leads some to being very loving.

Arabella:

I don't know those people, Jenny, and Cadwell would be of all men the one about whom I would least have it said.

Jenny:

They say he's the Don Juan of London.

Arabella:

Not mine.

Jenny:

Still, he has wit.

Arabella:

I find him somewhat silly—and the most annoying personality.

Jenny:

(interrupting her) He's well built.

Arabella:

What difference? I cannot stand him.

Jenny:

As for writing, nobody writes better.

Arabella:

What do you say? It's true that I haven't seen his letters, but then, as to his manners, I believe he's incapable of doing anything good.

Jenny:

Ah—I know of so many difficulties that cannot be arranged.

Arabella:

Eh! Who, Jenny?

Jenny:

What interest do you have in it?

Arabella:

I have some reasons for wishing to know it.

Jenny:

I have some, perhaps, for not telling you.

Arabella:

I beg you.

Jenny:

What do you care?

Arabella:

I would like to know who the unfortunate woman is who clings to him so mal apropos.

(Enter Lackey)

Lackey:

Selina asks to see you, madam.

Jenny:

(to Arabella) Hold—here exactly is one of the unfortunate women. (going to Laura's room)

(Exit Lackey and exit Jenny) (Enter Selina)

Selina:

You here all alone, madam?

Arabella:

As you see, madam.

Selina:

Where is Laura, madam?

Arabella:

I am waiting for her to wake up, madam.

Selina:

I must do the same, while I wait for my carriage to be sent over.

Arabella:

I have mine below—of which you may freely dispose.

Selina:

Could I do better than to be with you, madam?

Arabella:

I know people you would prefer easily enough.

Selina:

There's at least something I could tell you.

Arabella:

It's a little thing when one is instructed to the contrary. (Noticing the clasp on Selina) But what do I see?

Selina:

What do you see, madam?

Arabella:

I admire your pin. The diamonds are very nice. They're well set.

Selina:

You find it beautiful, madam? I am delighted that it is to your taste.

Arabella:

You've had it for some time, madam?

Selina:

A very long time, madam, but I rarely wear it.

Arabella:

(aside) Am I deceived? (looking at the pin) With your permission, madam. No, madam, it is not so long as you say.

Selina:

I tell you truly, madam.

Arabella:

I know what I say, madam.

Selina:

And I, madam, know when your questions begin to tire me.

Arabella:

But please, tell me how you got it.

Selina:

I don't have to give you an account of it.

Arabella:

Where did you buy it?

Selina:

Let's end this, if you please—

Arabella:

It must have cost you a lot.

Selina:

(noticing on Arabella the watch she sent to Cadwell) It cost me, madam, it cost me—more than you paid for your watch.

Arabella:

What balderdash are you giving me, madam? What has my watch got to do with the pin I spoke of?

Selina:

Madam, let's not enter further into an aggravating explanation. In these affairs the best way is to let things pass in silence. They are most unfortunate when discovered. In this adventure, at least, if we lose our lover, we at least get our jewelry back. I am going to return your pin—or I will keep it if you want to keep my watch.

Arabella:

No, madam, I don't wish to keep anything that would

give me the least reminder of the greatest villain in the world.

Selina:

(giving the pin) Here, madam, is your pin.

Arabella:

(giving the watch) And here's your watch.

(Enter Jenny)

Jenny:

What swap are you making? I want to see it.

Selina:

It's nothing, Jenny. (to Arabella) Goodbye, madam, I am going to take your carriage.

Arabella:

Don't keep it.

Selina:

I am not going far.

Jenny:

Madam is coming here.

Selina:

I just remembered something pressing.

(Exit Selina)

Arabella:

Your mistress is coming, you say?

Jenny:

I hear her.

Arabella:

I intend to avenge myself on the perfidy of Cadwell right away.

(Exit Jenny) (Enter Laura)

Laura:

Madam, I am in despair for having made you wait so long.

Arabella:

I've come to tell you something which will surprise you the most.

Laura:

Don't delay, madam, for I'm already impatient about—

Arabella:

(interrupting her) No, madam, if you please, this will be in front of Cadwell.

Laura:

What role does he have to play in what you have to tell me?

Arabella:

I intend to reveal to you what is in the heart of a man you esteem a little too much.

Laura:

(pointing to the door to Cadwell's apartment) Madam, there's the door to his apartment. (calling) Jenny, Jenny.

(Enter Jenny)

Jenny:

Madam?

Laura:

Tell Cadwell that madam (pointing to Arabella) wishes to speak to him.

Jenny:

Cadwell? He left more than an hour ago, madam.

Laura:

Fine! (Jenny exits) (to Arabella) I am not to know then, madam, what it is that is so important for me to learn?

Arabella:

Abuse me. No, madam, I repeat to you, Cadwell doesn't deserve any consideration from a person like you.

Laura:

You appear to me to be sufficiently well instructed, madam, and the manner in which you speak will begin to displease me if you continue to hide from me the reason—

Arabella:

Well, madam, learn to your shame and mine that Cadwell is deceiving us both; that he is the most villainous of men, and that having been disabused of his lies myself, I believe I ought to bring you out of your error.

Laura:

You oblige me much, madam, although a trifle late. You will permit me to say without getting angry that you would easily console me in my error if you were still in yours.

Arabella:

Cadwell easily made me believe all that he wished, madam. There are explanations between us, him, you, and me that—

Laura:

(interrupting her) Ah, madam, such explanations between three people are usually irritating. Avoid them, and give me without them all the proofs that you can of his infidelity.

Arabella:

You are going to see all of Cadwell, madam.

Laura:

(aside) Ah—inconstant man—

(Enter Bendish)

Bendish:

(aside, staying at a distance) They're talking about my master.

Arabella:

I will render you certain.

Laura:

(aside) Faithless!

Bendish:

That's him.

Arabella:

(pulling out a letter from her purse and presenting it to Laura) Here, madam. Read!

Laura:

(aside) Traitor! Infidel!

Bendish:

Oh, surely that's him. I recognize the epithets. Let's hear.

Arabella:

This is the only letter of the thirty or so he wrote me that I have kept. One of my women imprudently took the others from my drawer. Happily, I had this one about my person. It will suffice.

Bendish:

I believe we'll have to move a little sooner than we thought.

(Laura takes the letter and reads it to herself)

Arabella:

(after Laura has finished the letter) Well? What do you say to that, madam?

Laura:

Alas, madam, what can I say? I can say nothing.

Arabella:

You take this affair with plenty of moderation.

Laura:

Rumor is helpful.

Bendish:

(aside) Please God we may be rid of that rumor.

Arabella:

Adieu, madam.

Laura:

Madam, I bid you good day.

Arabella:

Aren't you going to give me back my letter?

Laura:

Please leave it here with me.

Arabella:

These sorts of things are not good in the hands of interested parties.

Laura:

It won't leave my hands.

Arabella:

Goodbye then, madam. (Seeing Laura is going to escort her out, and preventing it) Madam, where are you going?

Laura:

Madam, I leave you. It's just as well, I am in no condition—

Arabella:

(interrupting her) Go back in, then.

(Exit Arabella)

Bendish:

(aside) I can see it plainly. Our good fortune is going to cause us to flee to the country. Just heaven!

Laura:

(perceiving Bendish) Ah, Bendish, where is your master?

Bendish:

I believe he went to do something.

Laura:

Go tell him to come to me as soon as possible. As soon as possible, do you understand? Tell him that I have something to say to him of the utmost importance, that he come at once. Bring him with you. Do you understand clearly?

Bendish:

Yes, madam, I understand too well—and I haven't understood anything.

Laura:

Go then, quickly. Stay! I am going to write a word. That will hurry him more. I will do it in an instant.

(Exit Laura)

Bendish:

Ah, this blow will leave us lost without resources. May the plague choke coquettes, coquetry, and those who invented it. We are taken in a snare.

(Enter Cadwell)

Bendish:

Ah, sir.

Cadwell:

What's the matter with him?

Bendish:

You are lost.

Cadwell:

Really?

Bendish:

Sir, Arabella, that cursed Arabella, with arguments I don't understand— (hesitating to continue)

Cadwell:

Well?

Bendish:

She has given the letter you wrote her to Laura.

Cadwell:

Well?

Bendish:

Well? What more do you want? Don't you understand what followed?

Cadwell:

Well?

Bendish:

You're dreaming, I swear, with your "Well?"

Cadwell:

Well?

Bendish:

Well! Well! Well! Oh! And bad for you by all the devils in hell. Say something. At once.

Cadwell:

Wait here. I am going—

Bendish:

(interrupting him) She told me to look for you—

Cadwell:

Never mind, I'm going—I wish Arabella was dead.

Bendish:

Ha—how ugly she is now, right, sir?

Cadwell:

We must—

Bendish:

(interrupting him) Here's Laura.

(Enter Laura)

Laura:

(to Bendish without seeing Cadwell) Wait, Bendish, carry this to Cadwell. (seeing Cadwell) Ah, you here, sir. I am delighted to find you so apropos.

Cadwell:

Eh, madam! Did you think I was out again?

Laura:

I thought you were here—but henceforth—

Cadwell:

Today is not the day for you to make resolutions.

Laura:

Heaven grant I had never seen it. Monster that I look on with horror.

Cadwell:

I can tell from these epithets those who have been

inspiring you.

Laura:

And you can see from the effects the reward which is your due.

Cadwell:

I know that I should thank you for the indifference you have shown me for some time.

Laura:

Don't arrogate to yourself the scorn I intend to bear you for the rest of my life.

Cadwell:

You taught me yesterday that I must learn to expect it.

Laura:

Infidel! I have never passed a day without giving you some proof of my affection.

Cadwell:

Real affections, madam, that respond so ill to the urgings of my letter without any explanation. But let's not speak of that.

Laura:

What letter, perfidious one? What do you mean to say?

Cadwell:

Oh, let's stop talking. Spare me such names.

Laura:

No, no. I mean for you to explain yourself. I can justify myself very easily, and I will have some pleasure in doing so after the blackest, most cowardly— Continue once more. What letter do you wish to speak to me of?

Cadwell:

Oh, madam, what's the use of it? The letter Bendish gave you yesterday.

Laura:

To me?

Cadwell:

To you, madam.

Laura:

I received a letter?

Cadwell:

Uh, you yourself, madam.

Laura:

Which Bendish brought?

Cadwell:

He himself.

Laura:

That's not true.

Cadwell:

Bendish?

Bendish:

Sir?

Cadwell:

Didn't I write a letter yesterday?

Bendish:

Yes, sir.

Cadwell:

Didn't I tell you to take it to London?

Bendish:

That's true.

Cadwell:

To whom did you take it?

Bendish:

To whom?

Cadwell:

Yes, idiot! To whom? Wasn't it madam?

Bendish:

Yes, sir.

Cadwell:

Didn't you come express?

Bendish:

I remain in agreement.

Cadwell:

Didn't you enter this lodging to give it to her?

Bendish:

That's certain.

Cadwell:

Well—what did you do with it, you ass. Answer.

Bendish:

Sir.

Cadwell:

(interrupting him) You lost it, right?

Bendish:

Sir, when I came to madam's room to put it in her hands— (hesitating)

Cadwell:

Well?

Bendish:

I couldn't find it.

Cadwell:

Ah, fool! (to Laura) Madam, I beg your pardon. (to Bendish, pretending to menace him) I don't know what prevents me— (to Laura) I am in despair to have accused you so unjustly as I have done. (to Bendish) Find the letter, rogue! Was someone in the room?

Bendish:

There were a lot of people, sir.

Cadwell:

My letter will be lost! This is awful! In it I begged you to spend some time in the country with me and my aunt. And whoever has found it has used it to shred our relationship.— But please, madam, while I am unable to disguise the cause of my chagrin—explain to me what has aroused you so seriously against me.

Laura:

Oh, your dodge is very adroit, I admit. And I might be silly enough to believe you if your letter could agree with what you tell me. I have the letter. It is in my hands. I won't tell you how I got it. But let's see if you can explain away all the scorn it expresses for me.

Cadwell:

Scorn for you?

Laura:

Yes, cruel man—and in all its spite. (pulls out the letter) Listen. "I am in the country for the last two days and without Laura. The complaisance that I am obliged to show a sick aunt makes me stay in a strange solitude. Couldn't you try to render my condition supportable? If you do not take it on yourself, Laura and the whole world together cannot help me. I will never love and never adore anyone but you in my life. Adieu."

Bendish:

We shall see that someone counterfeited his signature. What will he say?

Cadwell:

Ah, I see now that no one poisoned you. I beg you, madam, give me the letter. (Laura hands it to him puzzled and he begins to read) "I am in the country for the last two days and I am without Laura! The complaisance that I am obliged to show a sick aunt makes me stay in a strange solitude. Couldn't you try to render my condition supportable? IF YOU DO NOT TAKE IT ON YOURSELF, LAURA—the whole world together cannot help me. I will never love and never adore anyone but you in my life. Adieu." (after having read the letter aloud) This letter is full of scorn for you?

Laura:

Oh, Cadwell, Cadwell, you have many enemies or I am very weak.

Cadwell:

Still something remains hidden. Madam, I beg you to explain. Let me know who I ought to challenge or distrust.

Laura:

No, Cadwell. Be content that I give no credence to the treason that I suspected of you.

Cadwell:

Madam, I am the happiest man in the world today—but innocence is always recognized. Yet I fear that mine in the end will succumb to some new imposture.

Laura:

Ah, Cadwell, can your interests be in better hands than mine? I am only too ingenious in finding reasons to excuse you, and my suspicions only begin when I cannot find you innocent.

Cadwell:

Yet, madam, what would have happened today, had I

not by a miracle understood and brought the truth to your eyes? I would have lost forever a heart that my fidelity ought to have preserved for me eternally. Can I be for a moment without mortal uncertainty in the future? Things pass through my head, each one more bizarre than the rest. I feel I'd rather not see you ever again in my life than to be so cruelly forsaken even once. Me—faithless to my dear Laura! Madam, if you don't assure me against all that can tempt you against me; if you don't promise to shut the mouths of those who slander me before you—you will see me die of despair.

Laura:

You don't love anyone but me, Cadwell?

Cadwell:

I hate all that is not you.

Laura:

Ah, Cadwell! Don't deceive me!

Cadwell:

Why would I do that, madam?

Laura:

How do I know? To pile conquest on conquest—to

satisfy a ridiculous vanity that all men pride themselves on these days. Such easy things don't do you honor, Cadwell.

Cadwell:

Ah, madam, I prefer to die.

Laura:

What are you doing today?

Cadwell:

Madam, my brother has asked me to visit him.

Laura:

Are you going?

Cadwell:

Soon, madam.

Laura:

When will I see you again?

Cadwell:

The very soonest I can.

Laura:

Adieu, Cadwell. Think of me.

Cadwell:

I am occupied by nothing but you.

(Exit Laura)

Bendish:

Well, sir, I'm learning, as you see.

Cadwell:

You did wonders.

Bendish:

Frankly sir, if you hadn't been seconded our ship would have come aground. Truly, the trouble that you had in this adventure—I'm not sorry it happened, for I don't doubt that after such a hot alarm you'll take care not to make another such mistake.

Cadwell:

(looking at his watch) What time is it? What the devil! Four o'clock. Sophia is waiting for me on the river.

Bendish:

Sir!

Cadwell:

Shut up!

Bendish:

(aside) Ah—what a man! (aloud) Shall I go with you?

Cadwell:

(taking a few steps towards leaving) No. (Returning) I forgot. (pulling a letter from his pocket and giving it to Bendish) Take this letter to the Duchess of Devonshire.

Bendish:

The Duchess of Devonshire? It's fifteen months since you last saw her.

Cadwell:

Go, I tell you.

Bendish:

(aside) What a devilish imagination. Ah, she sold land eight days ago. (aloud) I'm going. But where will I find you?

Cadwell:

At Charlotte's, where I must be precisely at five o'clock, don't you know? Don't wait, for I won't be long.

(Exit Cadwell)

Bendish:

Go, go, we are ordered. And by God, all is not going to end as it should. Cursed be the first little she-monkey that gave him his reputation. Really, what's so marvelous about him? Don't I have eyes, a nose, a body like him? It's chance that does everything. Just make a little stir and you will succeed in all things. The Duchess is amorous of so and so. She passes for a connoisseur. All the gallant ladies want to know if she's right. All try to please her. One by a veritable infatuation, another by jealousy, another by avenging a lover who had left her, to reawaken the ardors of a languishing lover—all to follow the fashion. For it's fashion in this as in all else. But let's go wait on her. For if I only need to deceive six persons for the remainder of the day, I'll be off quite cheaply.

CURTAIN

ACT III

The same, a short time later.

Worthy:

Sister, I've seen Victor, as you advised me. I was careful to tell him of Laura's attachment to Cadwell. Doubtless he's informed of what's happening, and I didn't think it would be honest for me to further agitate a man who seemed to be in despair. Besides, this is a bad way to earn the heart of a lady we esteem. But, sister, I believe chance has done for us all that we could hope. In short, Arabella, whom I just met, assured me that she has disabused Laura—that she had just put in her hands a letter from Cadwell—

Olivia:

A letter written by Cadwell to Arabella?

Worthy:

Yes, I tell you.

Jenny:

Ah, madam, how relieved I am! We are going to see the master and the valet greatly abashed. This puppy Cadwell, with his impertinent airs, and this rogue of a Bendish, who's starting to be like him. But listen, don't be fooled. Do what is necessary to finish things. If you give them time to repair the damage—

Olivia:

Ah, I don't know what to believe. Laura has a very cowardly heart—

Jenny:

My God, Laura loves him! Laura is credulous and Cadwell is a very loveable villain. You must dare all. Take her in a fit of passion or you will obtain nothing. As for me, I have taken the trouble to strengthen what you've told her, but I haven't noticed any change in the way she looks.

Worthy:

She's choking back her resentment. I have it from Arabella.

Olivia:

Go then, brother, go find her. Test her soul. Take advantage of such a favorable opportunity. And be sure something will happen. We are laying many traps for Cadwell. In the end they will enable us to open Laura's eyes.

Worthy:

Ah, sister, it's time that you do that, for truly, I am dying. This unjust prejudice for Cadwell is killing me. I really believe I would suffer less if he wasn't deceiving her.

Jenny:

What amuses you? You tell us here the finest things in the world. When you are with her you cannot open your mouth. If you saw Cadwell with Laura—he never stops talking, even if he repeats the same thing to her a hundred times.

Worthy:

He's happy, Jenny.

Jenny:

Go. Become him if you can.

(Exit Worthy)

Olivia:

But Jenny, the more I think of what my brother just

said, the less likely I think it.

Jenny:

I don't understand it any better than you. Cadwell was very gay when he left. Laura wasn't sad. There's a misunderstanding somewhere or Cadwell has played a trick of his specialty.

Olivia:

What could he have said against such strong proof?

Jenny:

My word, I don't know. What should I say to you? He opens his big eyes, he sighs, he threatens, he weeps, he falls to his knees, he walks about with long strides, breaks a chair, tears a ruffle, bites his nails, tears his hair, and in the end, he's right.

Olivia:

Nice manners to justify oneself!

Jenny:

If I hadn't seen him play the same role with her a thousand times, I wouldn't know what to say. He made me cry in the beginning, but now I am cured.— But you, madam, who speak as if you wish to help your brother, who can do it better than you? For I'm not blind. I've noticed for a long time that Cadwell watches you, and because I see that you respond well enough to all his tricks, I believe that you are not lacking in what it takes to prevail on his passion and undeceive Laura.

Olivia:

You have good eyes, Jenny. Well, since you have observed it, I am going to make you my confidant. It's something I've thought of for some time, but it's the last remedy I wish to employ, because I find it the most shameful.

Jenny:

Bah, madam, it is not shameful to punish a rascal.

Olivia:

Besides, I'm afraid he will distrust me.

Jenny:

Indeed! Him! He wouldn't distrust you if you told him you hated him. He is so sure of his own worth that he thinks people are forced to love him just by looking at him.— I hear someone. Perhaps it's him. He'll fall in any trap you set for him.

Olivia:

He's more clever than you can imagine.

Jenny:

If he didn't do foolish things, he wouldn't need all his trickery. It's for you to embroil him so well that nothing he can do will be enough to get him out of it.

Olivia:

Let me do it.

(Exit Jenny) (Then enter Cadwell)

Cadwell:

(with pretended embarrassment) I don't know what I ought to do, madam.

Olivia:

You must read your own thoughts and take counsel.

Cadwell:

Ought I to stay, madam, and expose myself to the greatest peril I have run in my life?

Olivia:

This enigma is very difficult to solve. But I do not see what peril you run in remaining here.

Cadwell:

Ah, madam, how badly my eyes serve me! That my sighs are so badly explained. What? All my actions have not made themselves understood?

Olivia:

I have only noticed in you that you are prodigiously at ease with the whole world.

Cadwell:

Ah, madam! If I haven't kept honest appearances for the others, much different are the ones I've had for you. You owe me a complete account of them. I have done it only to better hide my love.

Olivia:

Ah, Cadwell, are you thinking carefully of what you are saying to me?

Cadwell:

Yes, madam, I have thought of it. I know all that I risk. I know that I lose Laura forever if you abuse the sincere declaration I am making to you. But I know that I cannot live and hide my feelings for you.

Olivia:

I've seen too much of you to believe you are sincere.

Cadwell:

Eh! What do my feelings say to you, madam, who cannot be convinced by the strongest passion that ever was experienced?

Olivia:

Don't you swear that all the time to Laura?

Cadwell:

Judge by the continual reproaches I receive from her.

Olivia:

But you deceive her then?

Cadwell:

Why, madam, don't you know how things are done? Don't you know that an uncle ordered me to attach myself to her, and that her great wealth put this project in his head. I was not then engaged elsewhere. I consented to all he wished. But I saw you, madam, and love made me neglect a very considerable fortune.

Olivia:

Ah, Cadwell. I don't know if all you tell me is true. But I am sure I wish at least—

Cadwell:

(interrupting her and falling on his knees) Ah, madam! Permit me, I beg you, to throw myself at your feet. I conjure you in the name of the most lively tenderness of a passion which will never end to put me to the strongest test you can invent. Do you want Laura's letters? I abandon them to you. Do you want me never to see her again? I consent. Do you want me to smash her portrait before your eyes? I will do it. There's nothing I won't sacrifice. Command it!

Olivia:

I wish that you had never spoken.

Cadwell:

Had I offered you my first vows! I would still be faithful.

Olivia:

But Cadwell, what are you asking from me?

Cadwell:

That you love me, that you think it, and that you tell me—endlessly.

Olivia:

You will betray me.

Cadwell:

No, madam, never.

Olivia:

Put it in writing.

Cadwell:

In my blood, if necessary.

Olivia:

You no longer love Laura? You will live eternally for me? You promise me this, and your hand is ready to sign the declaration?

Cadwell:

Right now. Command me!

Olivia:

Don't forget then, Cadwell, to put in all that confirms your oaths.

Cadwell:

I am going to bring it to you, madam, while you in turn will give me proofs of your affection.

Olivia:

You will be content.

Cadwell:

That's enough.

Olivia:

I will wait for you.

(Exit Cadwell) (Then, enter Jenny)

Jenny:

Well, madam?

Olivia:

Everything's going fine. And my brother—what's he doing?

Jenny:

(seeing Laura enter with Worthy) Nothing much, madam.— Here he is.

(Enter Worthy and Laura)

Worthy:

What, madam! Nothing can dissuade you!

Laura:

Stop, Worthy. I know more about all that than you. It's as I told you.

Worthy:

The letter that Arabella gave to Laura—was a letter written to Laura.

Laura:

(to Olivia) That's the way it is.

Worthy:

(to Olivia) Arabella for inexplicable reasons takes the opportunity of using the letter to injure Cadwell.

Olivia:

Well, brother, the matter is doubtful. Laura loves Cadwell, she takes his side. What do you find extraordinary in that?

Laura:

The thing is not doubtful, madam. There are circumstances which assure me it is true.

Olivia:

(to Worthy) Madam's right. Show her he has deceived her so that Cadwell cannot deny it, then—

Laura:

(interrupting) Oh, I tell you if you can bring that about I will never see him again in my life.

Worthy:

But, madam, what more is necessary?

Olivia:

Oh, brother! How silly you are. (taking him to a nearby room) Come into this room, I want to talk to you.

Worthy:

But—

Olivia:

(interrupting him) I want to talk to you, I tell you. Follow me.

(Exit Olivia and Worthy)

Laura:

Ah, I've seen more than I want to see. They intend to hunt Cadwell out of my heart. They are taking measures to do it that will not succeed.

Jenny:

For that they are wrong, madam. For me, at present I am on his side. He tells you that he loves you—why not believe him? They suspect him wrongly. They say he deceives you—all the world believes it. What does it matter? You are the interested party—he made you listen to what he pleased, that's all. Must he render an account of his actions to others?

Laura:

My God, Jenny, I understand that language. But be advised that I am not a dupe. I have eyes like others—in an affair that was nobody's business but mine.

Jenny:

I am speaking seriously, madam. That young fellow loves you terribly.

(Exit Jenny, then enter Cadwell)

Cadwell:

Stay, madam—here—

Laura:

(interrupting him) What have you there? What do you intend to do with that letter?

Cadwell:

I am come to bring it to you, madam.

Laura:

May I see it?

Cadwell:

If you will bear with me. I must tell you the reasons that brought me to write it.

Laura:

I am listening to you.

Cadwell:

You must help me in this business.

Laura:

Speak quickly then.

Cadwell:

Madam, I can no longer stand all the nasty things said about us. I know that Olivia is part of it. I have decided to stop them, and I have found the way by pretending to make love to her.

Laura:

What?

Cadwell:

Listen, madam, here's the best part. From the first interview, I have so well advanced that we are come to terms.

Laura:

What are you saying?

Cadwell:

Hear the rest, I beg you. She has exacted a promise

from me that I will never love anyone other than herself. And she has even engaged that I must put in that I never loved you.

Laura:

You were able to write it?

Cadwell:

Pardon me for doing so. All appeared permissible to me to avenge you.

Laura:

And what can assure me that this pretense doesn't hide a truth?

Cadwell:

Everything, madam. And especially the care I have taken not to put this paper in her hands until you have seen it.

Laura:

Ah, Cadwell, I will never be able to accept such a pretense.

Cadwell:

Ah, madam, I beg you. Now I have the letter to Olivia

in my hands.

Laura:

Show me this paper.

Cadwell:

Madam, I hear Olivia. Contain yourself, I beg you.

Laura:

It will be hard.

Cadwell:

It must be done.

(Enter Olivia)

Laura:

Where have you come from, madam?

Olivia:

I've just come from a conversation with my brother which concerns you.

Cadwell:

(giving Olivia his letter) Madam, here's more than you asked me for. (Olivia takes the letter, reads it, and hands it to Laura) Madam, what are you doing?

Olivia:

Cadwell, do not be surprised if, after having deceived so many times, you are deceived in your turn. I never loved you and I have not the least jealousy—but I could no longer suffer you to trick a person who does not deserve your trickery. Besides, my brother's interest engaged me to all this. I am going to disclose your perfidy. But in the future, profit from this mischance. You have wit; mix in a little sincerity, and someday I hope you will thank me for the advice I have given you. (to Laura) Read, madam.

Laura:

(reading the letter to herself in a low voice) Cadwell.

Olivia:

(After Laura has finished reading) Well, what do you say to that?

Laura:

That I am delighted, madam, to know your good faith, and to be persuaded that you didn't wish to betray me.

Olivia:

You will continue to see Cadwell?

Laura:

Yes, madam.

Olivia:

You will continue to love him?

Laura:

More than I have ever done in my life.

Olivia:

Then I must never see you again!

(Exit Olivia)

Laura:

Cadwell, I must leave. (in a tone marked with rage) I cannot leave her much longer in her error.

(Exit Laura)

Cadwell:

What do you make of that? Laura doesn't appear to me much disabused. The uncertainty she was in when leaving me, her eyes which couldn't keep back some tears—all these things bode me no good. My shock at first would have betrayed me without a doubt. What does it matter? Well, so much the worse for her. I take every precaution possible to spare her chagrin. If she must chagrin herself, I consent. The trick I'm using is not true, but it's possibly true or so it appears to me, and she ought always to give me consideration for the trouble I take to try to deceive her.

(Enter Worthy)

Worthy:

Ah, my dear Cadwell, I am delighted.

Cadwell:

Eh! What for, Worthy?

Worthy:

By what they just told me.

Cadwell:

Eh! What have they just told you?

Worthy:

That you love my sister.

Cadwell:

It's true.

Worthy:

Oh, fine! I've come to assure you that nothing can prevent you from being happy together.

Cadwell:

Eh, how?

Worthy:

If you wish it, I promise you, I will employ all my credit with her to make her agree to marry you.

Cadwell:

I don't intend to get married.

Worthy:

What then?

Cadwell:

That's the way it is.

Worthy:

Didn't you tell me that you love my sister?

Cadwell:

I remain in agreement.

Worthy:

Uh—what do you intend by loving her?

Cadwell:

To love her.

Worthy:

Cadwell!

Cadwell:

Worthy!

Worthy:

You're not thinking of it.

Cadwell:

Pardon me.

Worthy:

You love my sister without thinking of marrying her?

Cadwell:

Do you marry all those you love?

Worthy:

There are certain men who ought not to love at all with ideas like that.

Cadwell:

That I intend to see.

Worthy:

You're losing your mind.

Cadwell:

I don't see anything peculiar about a man not wanting to get married.

Worthy:

Goodbye, Cadwell. You won't always be so happy or so clever.

(Exit Worthy)

Cadwell:

We shall see. God, this is funny. Once, I would have accepted the role, but after the trick his sister just played me—

(Enter Bendish)

Bendish:

Truly, you're prompt, I just came from Charlotte's—

Cadwell:

Peace!

Bendish:

I learned there that—

Cadwell:

Peace!

Bendish:

I went for your scarf—

Cadwell:

Shut up!

Bendish:

Your jerkin—

Cadwell:

Will you shut up!

Bendish:

(aside) Listen!

Cadwell:

Bendish?

Bendish:

Sir?

Cadwell:

Give me the mirror. (Bendish goes and returns with the objects as they are called for) Listen—my snuff box—wait—bring the armchair— Eh! My writing table.— No, give me a comb. Come on, then—will you hurry up?

Bendish:

Tell me exactly what you want—

Cadwell:

I don't know. I want to sit down. (aside) Madam Olivia, madam Olivia, you have played me at trick—

(Enter Jenny)

Jenny:

Madam wants to know if you sup here?

Cadwell:

Why, Jenny?

Jenny:

Because if you don't sup here she will go in town.

Cadwell:

I don't wish to constrain her, Jenny.

Jenny:

Eh! You don't constrain her as much as you think. Are you supping here or not?

Cadwell:

I will sup here if that will give her pleasure.

Jenny:

I will go tell madam.

(Exit Jenny)

Cadwell:

Do you know what has happened?

Bendish:

Nobody is speaking of anything else downstairs.

Cadwell:

But is Laura persuaded that the thing is as I wish her to understand it?

Bendish:

Apparently, since she wanted to know if you will sup with her.

Cadwell:

On my oath, this is really funny.

Bendish:

Very droll.

Cadwell:

Assuredly, she doubts nothing. What she has just sent to ask confirms that sufficiently. But finish. What did Caroline want with me?

Bendish:

That she never wants to see you; that she regards you at all times as a man without faith, without honor, slanderous, indiscreet, a traitor, rascal, unfaithful.

Cadwell:

Eh! What did you say?

Bendish:

I said nothing, sir. It was Charlotte. (pulling from his pocket a pair of gloves and presenting them to Cadwell) Still, she gave me a pair of gloves to oblige you to go there. (The Petite Chevalier appears) Wait —here's her nephew who has come to fetch you without a doubt.

(Enter the Little Gentleman)

Little Gentleman:

Eh! Good day, my friend.

Cadwell:

Eh, good day, child. Where are you going?

Little Gentleman:

I've come to see you. Are you angry about it?

Cadwell:

No, not at all. Hold on then.

Little Gentleman:

I intend to kiss you.

Cadwell:

(embracing him) Here's the way it's done.

Little Gentleman:

(embracing Cadwell a second time) And for my aunt, don't I get one?

Cadwell:

(retiring) Well—is it enough? Fie then, little trickster, you've ruined my wig.

Little Gentleman:

Yes, that's true. I made a big booboo. (to Bendish) Eh. Good day, Bendish. (presenting his hand to Bendish) Touch that.

Bendish:

(touching his hand) That's how it is done.

Cadwell:

Give him a seat.

Little Gentleman:

No. I don't know how to stay seated.

Bendish:

(to Cadwell) Can he be trusted?

Cadwell:

(to Little Gentleman) Come here.

Little Gentleman:

(throwing Cadwell's wig on the floor) Well?

Cadwell:

What a villain to father a child like this! Isn't it time to grow wise?

Little Gentleman:

And you who are much larger than I? My aunt says you are not very wise.

Cadwell:

Your aunt is crazy. Was it she who sent you here?

Little Gentleman:

She bet me half a crown that I wouldn't dare to come here to see if you were home.

Cadwell:

You made a bet?

Little Gentleman:

Certainly.

Bendish:

(aside) Plague. He knows. The little gossip has got him.

Cadwell:

(grabbing the Little Gentleman's nose) What have you got there? (making him take some tobacco) There.

Little Gentleman:

Ah, fie! Plague on the villain and his tobacco. Hold on, you will see if I don't tell my aunt.

Cadwell:

Will you shut up?

Little Gentleman:

Why'd you make me take tobacco then?

Cadwell:

Peace.

Little Gentleman:

If I don't make my aunt scold you.

Cadwell:

Little gallows bird.

Little Gentleman:

Patience.— You call my aunt crazy?

Cadwell:

Bendish.

Bendish:

Sir?

Little Gentleman:

When my aunt knows—

Cadwell:

Shut his mouth. He cries like a little demon.

Little Gentleman:

I will tell all this to my aunt.

Bendish:

Still?

Cadwell:

Bring him to me. (Bendish marches the Little Gentleman to Cadwell) My poor little man, I beg you. Don't make so much noise.

Little Gentleman:

You will see with your tobacco.

Cadwell:

Well, I won't give you anymore.

Little Gentleman:

If you hadn't done that, I would have told you something.

Cadwell:

What?

Little Gentleman:

No, you'll never know.

Cadwell:

I beg you.

Little Gentleman:

No.

Cadwell:

My little dear.

Little Gentleman:

No.

Cadwell:

Eh. The little animal doesn't see that I'm mocking him and that I know everything he intends to tell me.

Little Gentleman:

Yes? Do you know that my aunt told me to come here and to bring you to her, and that she told me to make it appear as if it came from me? But because of your tobacco you will know nothing. I know how to punish you.

Cadwell:

And I—I don't want to listen to you.

Little Gentleman:

And I—I have no desire to say anything further, either.

Bendish:

The good little messenger.

Cadwell:

Are my porters below?

Bendish:

Yes, sir.

Cadwell:

Follow me.

CURTAIN

ACT IV

The same, later that day.

Jenny:

Go on, go on, fear nothing. Laura is beginning to open her eyes. Our man will soon be taken, I tell you.

Worthy:

I am more afraid than ever.

Olivia:

Frankly, I have trouble persuading myself that your plan will succeed. All that's happened will make him more careful.

Jenny:

Him! It will make him more crazy. You don't know much about human nature. He's counting right now that he can make Laura believe black is white. Experience will only make him more bold. You will see if I don't know people.

Worthy:

If you can make me happy with your cunning, believe that—

Jenny:

Stop, you owe me nothing for whatever I do. I do it only because I want to do it. It's a natural bent I have to ruin all these little animals with beautiful manners and cold hearts. Ah, if all women were like me! I am furious when I think that they cause more honest men to be shunned, with their devilish jargon, their oaths, and endless tricks and rascalities. It puts me in a whopping rage.

Worthy:

Your man is warned.

Jenny:

He is instructed in what he must do.

Olivia:

He is not a man to be won over by money?

Jenny:

Oh, as to that, I cannot say. I don't know if the mediocrity of his fortune and the natural desire to acquire money wouldn't tempt him from an untested probity. But there is a remedy for that. Promise to pay him only if all goes well, and you will see that he will manage it.

Worthy:

As to that, Jenny, he can be assured. Where is he?

Jenny:

He's waiting in the Park for me to send for him.

Worthy:

I will go there myself.

Jenny:

You will do well.

(Exit Worthy)

Olivia:

I won't hide from you, Jenny, that I wouldn't get involved in this for anything or anyone but my brother. I don't like doing wrong.

Jenny:

You were not so scrupulous this morning.

Olivia:

I admit that and I don't know why.

Jenny:

I do.

Olivia:

Why?

Jenny:

You want me to say it?

Olivia:

Yes.

Jenny:

It's because he told you he loved you.

Olivia:

Yes, I admit it. If only his heart agreed with his manners.

Jenny:

(interrupting) Already more than half the way is taken. On my word, I thought I was speaking with a reasonable person, but I see that—

Olivia:

How you twist things around!

Jenny:

Eh! My God, I understand that talk, "his heart agreed with his manners." There's the jargon about which I was just speaking to you.

Olivia:

How crazy you are!

Jenny:

I am not crazy; I know what I'm talking about.

(Enter Laura)

Laura:

(to Olivia) Well, madam, again you bring me to the point of being disabused. Alas, when will you disoblige me by proving that Cadwell is unfaithful?

Jenny:

There's time remaining in the day.

Laura:

No, no, Jenny. Don't misunderstand. It's more than a day since I distrusted Cadwell. But can one separate so easily?

Olivia:

Listen, madam: for myself, I will say no more. An error which pleases—contents us; a different state would seem harsh. I don't wish to poison your life's peace.

Laura:

No, no, madam, let's finish it. It's time. I cannot remain for the rest of my life in the condition I am in. And I am tired of complaining.

Jenny:

Ah, that's better. Here's a woman. Courage, madam.

Laura:

I believe he's with Charlotte. Shall I send for him?

Jenny:

To what good? They are not going to tell you anything, and you will merely increase their happiness.

Laura:

Then do what you wish.

Jenny:

I will do only what I said. (Seeing Captain Slice appear) Here's Captain Slice. This is the man I spoke to you about.

(Enter Slice)

Laura:

Jenny has told you what must be done?

Slice:

Don't worry about anything, madam.

Jenny:

Have you some strong friends with you?

Slice:

I've got all I need.

Jenny:

Don't mess up, at least.

Slice:

Not my intention.

Olivia:

(aside) In truth, it makes me sad. (to Laura) Madam, yet once more— Don't push this any further. You will be unhappy.

Laura:

No, madam, I tell you I am dying of it.

Jenny:

(hearing someone) I hear someone on the little landing. Retire. Perhaps it's Cadwell. Oh, quickly. He mustn't see Captain Slice.

(Exit Laura, Olivia, and Slice) (After a moment enter Bendish)

Bendish:

Jenny, have you seen my master?

Jenny:

Bah! Silly, you know where he is better than I do.

Bendish:

No, may the Devil take me!

Jenny:

I just heard his porters.

Bendish:

It's true, but I was using them.

Jenny:

But why in a chaise? Were you ill?

Bendish:

Me? No. I wanted to make them earn their wages. I lost my master at the Opera. I don't know what has become of him. I believe one of his friends brought him home.

Jenny:

Ah, I hear him. Assuredly it is he. Goodbye.

Bendish:

Goodbye, my Princess. (exit Jenny) Pretty language. That's what you get from service—always learning something. My princess, my pretty lady, my little angel, my queen, my petite. Killing words like these and a few sighs, and behold, no more is needed to turn the heads of several ladies of my acquaintance.

(Enter Cadwell)

Cadwell:

(laughing) Ha, ha, ha, ha, ha!

Bendish:

What's making you laugh so?

Cadwell:

(still laughing) Ah, ah, ha, ha.

Bendish:

Tell me what it is, so I can laugh, too.

Cadwell:

I was at the Opera, as you know.

Bendish:

Indeed, you were there. What the devil do you want? You were in the pit, on the stage, in the balcony—there wasn't a place there you didn't get into.

Cadwell:

Didn't you see me in one of the wings?

Bendish:

Indeed, I saw you there, and I saw it when the house began to hiss you. They didn't hiss you like they do bad actors. If you persist, you will start a fashion of being hissed by spectators, fools, obviously. What the devil contortions were you making first on one foot, then the other?

Cadwell:

I was ogling a lady in the second balcony that I believe I know.

Bendish:

Do you call that ogling? Oh, at least I am not so gauche, now I know how to ogle. To shrug, turn one's head, kiss the tip of your gloves very tenderly, that's called ogling, right? Well, did she respond to this ogling?

Cadwell:

So well that I went up to her lodge, where I stayed but a moment with her because of a jealous husband who put his head through the curtain to find us. We didn't wait for him, so we went to another lodge where we watched him quarrel with a woman who had taken our original seats. I believe he even struck her with his fist. This caused such a disturbance that the music stopped. We didn't want to wait for the end of the adventure. So I took her home. Don't you find that funny?

Bendish:

Not at all. Of all this, I only like the ogling part. I intend to study under you. You seem to me to be an expert at this work.

Cadwell:

Me? I am only a school boy. I will show you a chap at the Opera who can put the whole stage down.

Bendish:

Isn't he the one who's always sweet, who believes all the ladies are in love with him, who gushes, sighs—and who can be heard from the back of the theatre.

Cadwell:

You've got him.

Bendish:

Ah, yes, I know him. Is he a lively fellow, too?

Cadwell:

He says so.

Bendish:

Is he rich?

Cadwell:

Why?

Bendish:

That's what I call lucky. Ah, I could be, too, since it's so easy. I intend to return to the Opera to ogle. (looking about him) Isn't there anybody here who likes ogling?

Cadwell:

Shut up, you are so stupid.

Bendish:

(hearing a knocking) Someone's knocking at the little stairway.

Cadwell:

Who can it be?

Bendish:

I don't know. Shall I see?

Cadwell:

See. At this hour I won't wait on anyone.

(Bendish goes to the door and after an instant returns)

Bendish:

They ask to speak to you and they want to know if you are alone.

Cadwell:

Who is this fellow?

Bendish:

He won't say. I've never seen him before.

Cadwell:

His name?

Bendish:

He won't say. Send him off, sir. For fear of a mischance. He doesn't look right.

Cadwell:

You say that you've never seen him before?

Bendish:

Right. But his mysterious demeanor, a pushed down hat, a cape that hides his nose—how the devil can I tell?

Cadwell:

Is it his cape or his face that doesn't look right?

Bendish:

Sir, there's talk of thieves. Suppose he's one?

Cadwell:

Aren't there two of us?

Bendish:

We are only one all the same.

Cadwell:

Do what I tell you.

(Bendish goes and returns with Captain Slice)

Bendish:

Enter, sir.

Slice:

Is it you, sir, they call Mr. Cadwell?

Cadwell:

Yes, sir.

Slice:

Can we be overheard?

Cadwell:

Not if you don't speak very loud.

Slice:

Would you please have your man retire?

Bendish:

(frightened and glad to go) Willingly.

Cadwell:

Stay! (to Slice) Sir, Bendish is discreet. One can say anything before him.

Slice:

It's a matter of some consequence.

Cadwell:

I hide nothing from him—

Slice:

If you like, but—

Cadwell:

(interrupting Slice) Sir, in that case, I prefer not to know what you have to tell me.

Slice:

As you prefer it thus, sir. In short, a widow lady of the finest quality—

Bendish:

(aside) I can breathe again. For this we have courage.

Slice:

A lady of quality, I tell you, wishes to meet you in an hour.

Cadwell:

Who is she?

Slice:

Far from telling you her name, sir, you will not speak to her except on certain conditions—which perhaps you will not accept.

Cadwell:

We must see.

Slice:

Will you permit yourself to be blindfolded while I take you to her? Also, permit your hands to be tied?

Cadwell:

Why all these precautions?

Slice:

Sir, she wishes it so. You have too much wit, sir, not to see as well as I that she intends to know the state of your heart before discovering herself to you. I say too much perhaps, and overstay my commission.

Cadwell:

Are you something to her?

Slice:

Sir, I have nothing to say to you about that.

Cadwell:

I know who it is.

Slice:

Perhaps.

Cadwell:

Is she a brunette?

Slice:

She could be.

Cadwell:

Large green eyes?

Slice:

Getting closer.

Cadwell:

Mouth neither large nor small?

Slice:

I say no more.

Cadwell:

Pretty hand?

Slice:

I won't reply.

Cadwell:

Admirable teeth? The nose— Come, come, my boy, I know who she is. (to Bendish) Bendish, she's the one at the ball. Yes, it's she for sure. (to Slice) Yes, my boy, I will go. Yes, I will go, I tell you. Oho, there my friend, admit to me that I have discovered her. Doesn't she lodge near the Arsenal? Eh? If you please? Oh, I will go on my word. I've figured her out, right?

Slice:

(hesitating to respond) Sir.…

Cadwell:

Oh, you are stupid, my poor heart, I am more clever than you. In what direction? At what time? You haven't said.

Slice:

In an hour. From wherever you wish.

Cadwell:

In the Palace Courtyard, in half an hour.

Slice:

No, that's too soon.

Cadwell:

Well, in an hour.

Slice:

That's fine.

(Exit Slice)

Cadwell:

It's Lady Julia—without a doubt.

Bendish:

Oh, I believe it. But didn't you promise to have supper with Laura?

Cadwell:

I will return. That doesn't worry me. What worries me is what I will do here for another hour. (looking at his watch) It's not yet— For me, I cannot remain here a minute longer. I have to do something.

Bendish:

The time you employ doing nothing is the time you employ the least badly.

Cadwell:

And you—you never are more witty than when I tell you to shut up. (Making Bendish examine his face) Tell me—how do I look? This jerkin appears to me to have a short waist. What do you think?

Bendish:

Effectively—I don't know. Yes, you're right.

Cadwell:

Give me another.

Bendish:

Which one?

Cadwell:

Whichever you please. Bring me the one I wore yesterday.

Bendish:

Fie!

Cadwell:

Why?

Bendish:

It won't go well with you. Keep this one.

Cadwell:

I don't like it.

Bendish:

The other one makes your shoulders too large.

Cadwell:

Never mind.

Bendish:

When you want something, you want it.

Cadwell:

What talk! Are you going?

Bendish:

(hesitating to reply) Sir?

Cadwell:

What?

Bendish:

You are going to be angry with me.

Cadwell:

What's the scamp trying to say? Are you going to give me my jerkin?

Bendish:

(half crying) Sir.

Cadwell:

Well?

Bendish:

I spilled tallow on it trying to clean it.

Cadwell:

Where is it?

Bendish:

I took it to have the grease taken off before I brought it back.

Cadwell:

Go get it right away.

Bendish:

Sir, it won't be ready.

Cadwell:

Bring it to me in whatever condition it is.

Bendish:

Sir.

Cadwell:

What now? Will you go?

Bendish:

Sir.

Cadwell:

What now? Will you go?

Bendish:

Sir, I must tell you the truth. I loaned it to a student for a tragedy.

Cadwell:

My jerkin to a college boy? To a child?

Bendish:

No, sir. He's a big fellow, handsome, well-made—like you—and he plays the king in a tragedy.

Cadwell:

Ah, truly, I am pleased to know that you loan my clothes. But the moment this tragedy is finished, get it back the very instant. (Seeing Bendish hesitate) What then? You won't do what I tell you?

Bendish:

(hesitating) Sir?

Cadwell:

Ah, I see what it is. You put it in pawn, correct?

Bendish:

Sir, you've divined it. As you never give me my wages or advance money to me, I've had recourse to prompt expedients.

Cadwell:

You will pay me for this, I promise you. Give me the red one, Bendish. (Bendish goes into Cadwell's room) But look at this little scoundrel. Put my clothes in pawn.

Bendish:

(returning with a red jerkin and presenting it to Cadwell) Here it is.

Cadwell:

(not putting on the jerkin that Bendish brings him but asking for different garments, as soon as they are brought) Ah, I know how to live, I assure you. Another wig. I will teach you to play such tricks. Another hat! But just watch and see, I beg you. A mirror. Who has ever heard of such a thing. A scamp that I have showered benefits on. The orange flower.— To abuse me so easily. Ah, you don't know me yet, I see that clearly. A handkerchief. You will repent, mark my words.

(listening to rapping) Go open up. You will see a little the difference there is.

(Bendish opens the door and introduces Mr. Martin)

(Enter Martin, holding a scarf)

Bendish:

Mr. Martin, your scarf—

Cadwell:

Ah, Mr. Martin, your servant. You see me in a rage.

Martin:

Sir, it's not my fault.

Cadwell:

(to Bendish) Will you take this mirror? (Bendish holds the mirror for him)

Martin:

I've come—

Cadwell:

I am very glad to know you—

Martin:

I'm in despair—

Cadwell:

(to Bendish) I just remembered.

Martin:

I must tell you—

Cadwell:

(to Bendish) A cad—

Martin:

(astonished) Sir!

Cadwell:

An insolent—

Martin:

Sir!

Cadwell:

An impudent.

Martin:

Sir.

Cadwell:

A rogue, a cheat—

Martin:

Oh, sir!

Cadwell:

Don't you see that I am talking to this scoundrel!

Bendish:

(low to Martin) Want to be in it for half?

Martin:

(low to Bendish) No, I won't play such a rotten game.

Cadwell:

(to Bendish) I believe you are joking.

Bendish:

(pointing to Martin) Ask if I haven't spoken—

Cadwell:

(to Martin) There, let's see. Do you have my scarf?

Martin:

(displaying the scarf) Here it is.

Cadwell:

(examining it) It's very pretty. How much did you pay him?

Martin:

This morning a masked lady in a chaise came to my shop to purchase it from me. It was only ten o'clock. I believed that you would not be awake. Another lady, also masked, paid my wife for it. My wife went out. A third purchased it from my daughter. What shall I do with this money? I don't know who gave it to me?

Cadwell:

Make me two more scarves.

Martin:

Same kind?

Cadwell:

No, different. You have some wit, to adjust things like that.

Martin:

Fine, sir, you will have them in the morning.

(Exit Martin)

Bendish:

Sir, in favor of so many scarves, won't you pardon me for a little jerkin?

Cadwell:

I will pardon you, but if ever in your life—I am going to spend a few minutes with this little shop girl near here, waiting for the hour.

Bendish:

Shall I go to find you?

Cadwell:

No, I have no need of you. I must be alone. Didn't they say that?

(Exit Cadwell)

Bendish:

Plague! At least I wasn't so stupid as to give him the jerkin he asked for! It's a lucky jerkin for lucky men. They usually are employed in great matters, and I intend to use it in a great affair. For once in my life I intend to know what it is to be a man of fortune. I already know how to ogle; as for small talk I know that. I have only to dress quickly. (taking Cadwell's clothes from an armoire, and dressing with difficulty, for Cadwell's clothes are a bit tight) Oh, let's begin with this divine jerkin. Plague! It's tight. Oh, who cares! A snip with the scissors and two or three stitches with a needle are no great matter. All right, hips—get smaller. No good. What's the difference? I will say that they brought it this way. You will see that I will start a fashion of high hips. I have been seen before with big shoulders and elbows in arrears. Here's a jerkin which seems very easy for me to put on. These cursed tailors put the buttons so far from the button holes, I will burst. Well, who would not suffer for good luck. Was ever a man better dressed? Large head, small waist, low hips. Dammit, I intend to forget that Cadwell exists. Damnation, I almost forgot the best part. Orange flower water. Can one have good fortune without orange flower water? (he takes a flask from the toilet and sprays himself) It seems to me I have all the attributes of a lucky man. God protect us from mishap!

CURTAIN

ACT V

The same, an hour later.

Jenny:

Where the devil is Olivia? Where is Worthy? Worthy hasn't returned yet. What is all this? On my oath, I am going crazy? I take this business to heart worse than if it were my own.

(Enter Worthy)

Jenny:

Eh! Where are you coming from?

Worthy:

I've been to Arabella and then Selina.

Jenny:

To do what?

Worthy:

To bring them to witness the comedy. Didn't you tell me it was necessary for them to be present to prevent Laura from relapsing?

Jenny:

Yes, but it's more important to know if the comedy is going to go on.

Worthy:

Since Slice hasn't returned, all is going well. He's thought of everything, without a doubt.

Jenny:

(derisively) Oh, there, there, everything's going fine. Nothing could spoil it.

Worthy:

What's Laura doing?

Jenny:

Oh, my word. She's quite resolved never to see Cadwell again if he falls into the trap.

(Enter Slice)

Slice:

Sir?

Worthy:

Ah, you here? Well?

Jenny:

What have you done?

Slice:

He's undoing himself. He's sure he knows the imaginary person I told him of. I didn't want to undeceive him, since he's so sure of it.

Jenny:

He's going to let you blindfold him?

Slice:

Everything, I tell you.

Jenny:

Ah, the funny dodo. His name will become famous.

Slice:

He will meet me in the Park in a few minutes.

Worthy:

It isn't far. Better for you to wait for him. Hurry! Have you a carriage?

Slice:

I've everything that's necessary.

Jenny:

If by chance he tries to tear off his blindfold?

Slice:

Don't worry about anything. Two of us will prevent him.

Jenny:

Get going, then.

(Exit Slice, then enter Laura and Olivia)

Laura:

(to Jenny) Well—is he coming then?

Jenny:

Yes, madam.

Laura:

On the conditions imposed on him?

Jenny:

Yes, madam.

Laura:

I have trouble believing it.

Worthy:

It's your tenderness speaking for him again, madam.

Laura:

Don't speak of tenderness anymore, Worthy. But permit me to doubt what I haven't seen.

Worthy:

Do you really need this additional proof, after all that has passed?

Laura:

My God, Worthy, I am not taking his side. But still all that's happened doesn't absolutely prove he's guilty.

Olivia:

My brother always persists at the wrong time.

Laura:

Not at all, madam, and we cannot both be right.

Jenny:

The silly goose will not give up his intrigues.

Laura:

Shut up, Jenny. These jokes don't please me, understand?

(Enter Arabella and Selina)

Laura:

Ah, ladies, I am delighted to see you here. You couldn't come at a better time.

Arabella:

(to Laura) Why, madam?

Selina:

Eh? How's that, madam?

Jenny:

We are going to trap a goose. Don't say anything.

Laura:

(to Arabella) And above all, you, madam.

Arabella:

If it's something regarding Cadwell, as Worthy told me—(pointing to Selina)—this lady can take a greater part than I.

Olivia:

Selina is also a rival of Laura's?

Selina:

Me? I don't know what they're talking about?

Jenny:

Come, come, madam, admit the debt. There's no one here Cadwell has not deceived.

Worthy:

Truly, it merits a public punishment.

Laura:

You don't take it badly, sir. But if things don't work out as you plan, won't his glory be greater?

Selina:

I don't know what to say about it at all.

Olivia:

(pulling Selina into a corner) I am going to instruct you, madam.

Laura:

But, madam, if Cadwell doesn't come, what good is it?

Jenny:

Well! What a misfortune! Madam is not an interested party?

Arabella:

(going to Selina and Olivia) I intend to know all about this, too. They've told me quite imperfectly.

(The three talk)

Laura:

(to Worthy) Worthy, the hour's passing. Cadwell, isn't coming. I admit to you that I won't be angry if he makes fun of you.

Worthy:

At least I will have the consolation of knowing he deserves the tenderness you have for him, madam. But I don't see anything to make you hopeful. It is not yet time.

(Olivia, Arabella, and Selina join Worthy and Laura)

Arabella:

(to Olivia) Really, this is very pleasant.

Olivia:

Will he be stupid enough to chance it?

Jenny:

Oh, indeed yes.

Laura:

I doubt it, Jenny. A man with the character you ascribe to him would be more careful.

Jenny:

Unless another woman holds him off, I cannot conceive what would restrain him.

Laura:

Worthy, he's not coming. (to Olivia) Madam, he's not coming. (To Selina) Madam, do you believe he will come?

Selina:

I truly don't know, madam.

Jenny:

At the beginning, didn't he keep every rendezvous you gave him?

Selina:

Oh, shut up, Jenny. I am angry with myself.

Olivia:

(hearing someone enter) I hear a noise.

(Enter Slice)

Slice:

Snuff the lights.

(Jenny snuffs the lights)

Laura:

(aside) I am lost.

Slice:

My men are keeping him in the antechamber. Shall he be brought in?

Laura:

Yes, let him come in. I intend to see him. Who will speak to him? I admit I lack the strength to do it myself.

Worthy:

Is there need to speak to him? Aren't you satisfied, madam? Besides, he knows your voice.

Jenny:

Doesn't he know the voices of all the ladies here? By heart, by all the devils! This is the worst of it. Wait—I can change my voice. Let him enter. Do you wish it, madam?

Laura:

Do what you wish.

(Slice brings in Bendish dressed like his master, blindfolded)

Slice:

(to Bendish) We are entered into her apartment. You have only to wait to be happy.

Bendish:

I've been here before, my boy. I assure you that it is only out of consideration for you, and because I don't wish you to lose your promised reward, that I am not at this very moment calming two irritated mistresses.

Slice:

I am much obliged to you. Remember, that the least effort you make to see madam may cost you your life.

Bendish:

Oh, I am not worried. Come, come, my friend, I am accustomed to these types of adventures, and we have brought off more perilous ones than this.

Slice:

You are at present in her boudoir, and I leave you alone with her.

Jenny:

(low to all but Slice and Bendish) Silence, don't make the least noise.

Bendish:

(aside) Watch out for trouble!

Jenny:

(aside) Nice beginning.

Bendish:

Well, angel, here I am.

Laura:

(aside) The traitor!

Jenny:

Keep such sweet talk for when you know me better. Listen before responding to the things I have to say to you.

Bendish:

Plague! You take me for a great fool! I intend to prove to you I merit the choice your heart has made. For I believe you didn't send for me to tell me you hate me.

Jenny:

You won't know my true feelings if you don't clear up the uncertainty I am in at once.

Bendish:

Come, my little heart, my queen, let's not amuse ourselves with twaddle. Look at these stooping airs, this figure. When we know each other a little better I will ogle you.

Laura:

(aside) This cannot be Cadwell!

Arabella:

(aside, half voice) No, surely not.

Bendish:

Who just said I am not Cadwell? You lied.

Olivia:

(low to Worthy) Brother, it isn't him.

Worthy:

(low) I don't know what to make of it.

Selina:

(low) It's not him.

Jenny:

(to Laura in a half voice) Madam, it's Bendish.

Bendish:

What do you mean, Bendish? Who's that, then, my little friend?

Jenny:

(low to Laura) It's him, madam.

Worthy:

(half voice) A stick.

Bendish:

What do you mean a stick? Madam, I will dishonor you.

(Jenny looks for and finds a stick)

Worthy:

Quickly!

(Jenny beats Bendish with the stick)

Bendish:

(trying to get off his blindfold) Assault! Again? Oh, murder. They're trying to assassinate me.

Worthy:

What, rogue! Are you playing with us?

Laura:

Well, wasn't I right? Come Worthy, stop deluding yourself. Cadwell loves me and to mock you better he sends his valet. (to Arabella and Selina) What do you say, ladies?

Arabella:

I say it isn't astonishing, for he's never been caught in his life.

Laura:

(to Selina) And you, madam?

Selina:

That he will repent.

Olivia:

(to Laura) For myself, I say nothing.

Jenny:

And I, I always said he was a clever cheat.

Worthy:

There's something in this that I don't understand, but I will soon find out. (To Bendish) Will you talk?

Bendish:

(hesitating) Sir?

Worthy:

Come on, quickly.

Bendish:

(still hesitating) Sir?

Worthy:

(putting his hand on his sword and menacing him) I will kill you.

Bendish:

(throwing himself on his knees) Spare a lucky man.

Worthy:

Come on, now, admit it. What do you say about all this?

Bendish:

(hesitating and getting up) Whatever you wish, sir.

Worthy:

Well?

Bendish:

The curiosity to be a lucky man and the ease that I found in playing the role of one, made me try—as you see.

Worthy:

Ah, rogue! And how did you do it?

Bendish:

I told my master the rendezvous was changed to ten p.m. and I came at nine in his place.

Worthy:

Then it still isn't ruined. It's not quite ten o'clock. Slice, go back to the Park. You've taken the valet for the master. You will find Cadwell— Bring him as you did this one.

Slice:

If I find him, I will be back here in no time.

(Exit Slice)

Worthy:

Madam, Cadwell will not be so faithful as you imagine.

Laura:

(to Bendish) Bendish, do you think he will come?

Bendish:

Madam, I don't know anything about it. But if in my life, I get lucky—

Jenny:

(interrupting him) Things don't always succeed.

Bendish:

Experience makes me doubt a bit. But at least I know the rap that rapped me so distinctly. If it's this little rapper, she's devilishly strong.

Jenny:

It was me. I ought to have done it to you a long time ago.

Bendish:

I thank you for your favors.

Arabella:

(to Laura) If Cadwell's going to come, we won't be long in knowing. The Park isn't far from here.

Selina:

I will be very irritated not to see the end of this adventure, although I preferred him to a person who wasn't very disagreeable.

Laura:

(to Jenny) Jenny, see if someone isn't coming down there.

Bendish:

I will go to hurry him if you wish, madam.

Worthy:

(to Laura) Madam, don't let him leave, if you please.

Laura:

(to Jenny) Someone's coming now.

(Jenny goes to the door)

Bendish:

(aside) I see that he won't be here too soon.

Jenny:

(returning) Madam—(to Laura)—our man sent me to tell you he will be here in a moment. He's taking several detours so he cannot judge the distance.

Laura:

Come on, it's over. I will be absolutely cured, and I think I will never speak to him again in my life.

Selina:

Although you'd like a confession from me, know that I

have more fortitude than you, and that I have forgotten him more easily than I came to love him.

Arabella:

As for me, I haven't got such a strong soul.

Selina:

(to Olivia) But you, madam, he loves you.

Olivia:

Like the others.

Bendish:

I assure you that you are the only woman in the world of whom I never heard him say a bad thing.

Laura:

And of me, Bendish?

Bendish:

Oh, for you, he loves you, madam.

Laura:

Who can doubt it after this? I am going to speak to him myself. I won't bother to change my voice.

Worthy:

Madam.

Laura:

(interrupting him) I beg you, let me do it. I intend to speak to him. (to Olivia, Arabella, and Selina making them sit in a corner) Ladies, be seated. (to Worthy, also placing him to the side) Worthy, you sit back, too.

Worthy:

Tell Bendish to be silent.

Bendish:

I don't intend to say a word. (to Laura) Do you treat all lucky men the way I was treated?

Laura:

It is only a traitor who deserves it, a liar like your master.

Bendish:

I will have my revenge.

Jenny:

(low to Laura, leading in Cadwell) Madam, here he is.

Laura:

Everybody retire.

(All go to their places. Jenny and Bendish beside each other. Enter Cadwell blindfolded.)

Laura:

(to Cadwell in a disguised voice) Here's an adventure that resembles those in a novel. Sir, I believe you won't find the precautions I have taken bad. Your reputation is bad enough as regards women so that I cannot see you otherwise. Nature, which perhaps has not protected me very well, engages me to know the state of your heart before disclosing mine. Some attentions paid to me persuade me that I am pretty, that I have wit, that I am always done justice. I've never found it in me to make a man unfaithful to his beloved. Even when my vanity flatters me to the point of making me believe I could, the goodness of my heart dissuades me from doing it. My pleasures do not augment from the shame of others. Nor does a false one cease to be false. Speak then sincerely, if you can. Are you free?

Cadwell:

You will judge my sincerity by the confession you are about to hear. I don't have a free heart, madam. I don't wish to deceive you: I'm in love and I have been for a long time. You see at least that my behavior gives the lie to the reputation ascribed to me.

Worthy:

(low to Olivia) He recognizes her.

Olivia:

Shut up.

Laura:

You love, Cadwell? For a long time you say?

Cadwell:

Yes, I love, madam. And with a love that will end only with my life.

Laura:

But this so tender love—isn't it offended by the steps you are taking?

Cadwell:

I will have a hard time telling you what made me come here.

Laura:

Really, I don't know how to stop myself from praising

you. If I cannot win you, at least I have the pleasure of knowing you are not such as you have been painted. But Cadwell, can I obtain the bounty from you at the price of my tenderness?

Cadwell:

There's nothing I wouldn't do for you so long as it doesn't injure my passion.

Worthy:

(low to Selina) He recognizes her, I tell you.

Selina:

(low) Eh, shut up.

Laura:

(to Cadwell) I wouldn't want you to do such an extraordinary thing. I don't want to find you even indiscreet. But Cadwell, if I divine your mistress, I want you to admit it to me. Is it Arabella?

Cadwell:

Ah, madam, of whom are you talking to me?

Laura:

What makes you recoil so strongly? Has she no merit?

Cadwell:

Ah, madam, let's not discuss Arabella in detail. We will find so little of nature, and so many things borrowed. Please, madam, let's not talk of it any more. There are some people that should never be spoken of.

Arabella:

(low to Selina and almost rising) I don't know how I can hold back.

Selina:

Wait till the end.

Laura:

(to Cadwell) There's a rumor all over the place that you love Selina.

Cadwell:

She's a madwoman.

Bendish:

(to Worthy) That pays her off.

Laura:

Oh, I have divined it. It's Olivia who lives with Laura.

Cadwell:

Oh, madam do you know her? Distrust her. She's got the most wicked disposition.

Laura:

Name her yourself then?

Cadwell:

Ah, madam, if you knew her as I do, you would easily pardon my insensibility to you.

Laura:

Is she witty?

Cadwell:

Yes, madam, she is that. But no part of her wit is not fully grown. It seems that hers only serves to discover it in others.

Laura:

Why that's a pretty character indeed. She's beautiful without a doubt.

Cadwell:

Ah, don't engage me to paint her portrait. I couldn't do

it without offending you. And you, never having seen her, I cannot tell you how I find her the most adorable woman in the world.

Laura:

(sighing) She ought to be content to appear so to your eyes.

Cadwell:

(trying to take off his blindfold) Let's not pretend further and permit me the joy of seeing the only person with whom I wish to live.

Laura:

(stopping him) Stop!

Cadwell:

Eh, madam, what good are all these delays? I know you, I know who you are.

Laura:

Wait. To whom do you think you are speaking?

Cadwell:

To you, madam.

Laura:

I am not Laura.

Cadwell:

And it isn't to her that I address my vows. And I must tell you only the hope that it could be Lady Julia made me come here. If it isn't to her that I speak, I shall return without seeing you.

Laura:

You don't love Laura anymore?

Cadwell:

No, madam, I never loved Laura.

Laura:

You don't love me, liar! You dare to say that to my face! Eh! Why did you deceive me then? (tearing off his blindfold)

Bendish:

This isn't funny unless accompanied by blows from a stick. That would be much more pleasant to me.

Arabella:

Goodbye, Mr. Cadwell. I thank you for the kind sentiments you have for me.

Olivia:

(to Cadwell) As for me, I am satisfied.

Selina:

Adieu, Cadwell.

Jenny:

(to Bendish) Adieu, Mr. Bendish.

Laura:

(to Worthy) Mr. Worthy, will you take my hand?

Worthy:

Will I indeed!

Laura:

I give it to you. (to Cadwell) Adieu, false one. Don't ever see me again.

(Exit Laura, Worthy, Olivia, Arabella, Selina, Slice, and Jenny to Laura's apartment.)

Bendish:

Come, sir! Hadn't we better be on our way? We will soon be evicted. Above all, let's change our names and the part of town we live in. We are denounced hereabouts like counterfeit money.

Cadwell:

(aside, overwhelmed with astonishment and confusion) Just Heavens!

Bendish:

If this would only teach him—

CURTAIN

ABOUT THE TRANSLATOR

Frank J. Morlock has written and translated many plays since retiring from the legal profession in 1992. His translations have also appeared on Project Gutenberg, the Alexandre Dumas Père web page, Literature in the Age of Napoléon, Infinite Artistries.com, and Munsey's (formerly Blackmask). In 2006 he received an award from the North American Jules Verne Society for his translations of Verne's plays. He lives and works in México.

www.ingramcontent.com/pod-product-compliance
Lightning Source LLC
LaVergne TN
LVHW040115080426
835507LV00039B/372